SIXTH DAY

BRADFORD TROLLEYBUSES
THE END OF THE ROAD

INTRODUCTION

Bradford was the first and last trolleybus operator in Britain. Much has been written about the history so repetition is unnecessary. Here is a selection of previously unpublished photographs of the ever-changing city centre which has mostly vanished, and of the suburbs where time has (almost) stood still.

This volume illustrates the final few years of trolleybus operation. Several routes had already been converted by the time I had the funds for colour photography (which wasn't cheap in the 1960's), and Bradford's weather frequently made colour photography a rather pointless exercise!

All photos in this volume were taken by the Author.

Stan Ledgard
2010

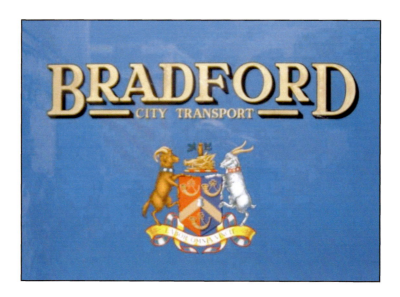

Front Cover: 712 speeds up Allerton Road from Four Lane Ends, having worked a service to Spring Head Road and now heading to Duckworth Lane depot via Squire Lane.

SIXTH DAY

Continuing with the theme of working 'on the buses', as in my previous Bradford trolleybus books, the normal working week was of five days. If you were lucky, you might find an overtime duty on one of your days off. This was called 'Sixth Day'. If you were very, very lucky and a real workaholic, you might grab a duty on your other day off, this being called 'Seventh Day'.

SALTAIRE AND GREENGATES 40/42

The longest trolleybus routes from the City at this time was route (40) Saltaire, running from Bolton Road (adjacent to Forster Square) to Bolton Junction, Five Lane Ends, where the (42) Greengates diverged, Thackley, Shipley and to Saltaire roundabout.

831 turns into Bolton Road to work a trip to Greengates. Forster House provides the backdrop. Nothing in this picture remains in 2009.

At the other end of the route, 742 arrives at Saltaire where she will turn on the roundabout outside Saltaire depot. On the left 776 departs for Bradford. Above the vehicles is the reversing triangle into Dove Street (on the right).

Looking the other way, 795 arrives as 799 departs. Both were former St Helens trolleybuses. Saltaire roundabout is in the distance.

Despite the fact that there were no frogs, crossings or optional routes for trolleys through Shipley, it proved a photogenic locality. Descending to the railway bridge, 735 passes the disused Shipley (Great Northern) station from which trains ran to Bradford Exchange via Thackley, Idle and Eccleshill.

Near Fox Corner, 831 has failed and is about to be passed by a West Yorkshire on the Leeds-Keighley service and the next trolleybus heading for Saltaire.

Left
775 creeps under the railway bridge at Shipley, her booms offset over the pavement because of the low clearance.

Below
Approaching from Saltaire, a trolley cautiously negotiates the curves in Briggate, Shipley.

Right
A trolley from Saltaire is about to pass under the bridge at Shipley. In the foreground is Bradford Beck, a former Stygian watercourse.

Below
At about the same place, 847 emerges from the bridge, heading for Saltaire. The Beck is over the parapet on the right.

833 makes a dash from Shipley. The market clock tower stands out in the background.

Sister vehicle 834 coasts in to Salts village.

831 turns on to the roundabout at Five Lane Ends, running from Saltaire.

847 from Greengates leaves the roundabout towards Bolton Road.

A trolleybus speeds up Bolton Road, escaping the City mists.

Bolton Junction after removal of the Eccleshill wires. It still looks complicated !
A trolleybus turns from Five Lane Ends towards City.

At Saltaire, an Atlantean demonstrator arrives under the Crossflatts wires.

After some shunting around it is parked in the depot yard next to trolleybus 779 which is taking a break on service 40.

ALLERTON 16

Route 16 City-Allerton (Stoney Lane) was a leisurely route to the point of being boring. It was the first of the Duckworth Lane depot routes to be axed. Here 841 basks in winter sun at the Stoney Lane terminus.

705 passes the bottom of Squire Lane and turns down West Park Road. Joining from the left are the Four Lane Ends wires, and from the right are those from Squire Lane. Behind is the Metal Box Company building.

To or from Duckworth Lane Depot, trolleys could travel via Squire Lane to routes 7 and 16. Outbound this included a trip down West Park Road, as demonstrated here by 844.

A view from the top of West park Road, looking over the allotments to Thornton Road, where a trolley (centre of picture) is bound for Four Lane Ends. The lighter-coloured building in the background is AIS, Ingleby Road, and there is still a sprinkling of mill chimneys.

Latterly the vehicles based at Duckworth Lane Depot (Routes 7, 8, 16) were all front entrance. Thornbury, which supplied all other routes, had a very mixed fleet. Their ex-St Helens 796 waits patiently at Tong Cemetery.

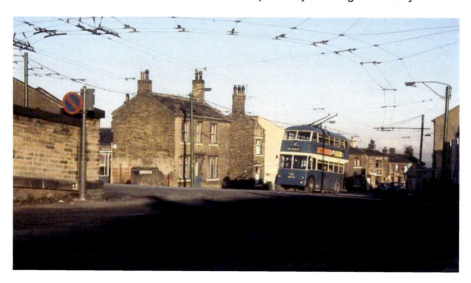

On the other hand 745 (revived after years in store at Thornbury) speeds away across the Little Horton turning circle at the bottom of St Enoch's Road, en route to Wibsey.

CITY

Alterations at the bottom of Thornton Road have begun. 716 stands at the Clayton barrier. Driver-trainer motorbus 061 passes the rubble where Provincial House is to be built.

713 on service 37 leads 703 on service 7. A motorbus on route 5 tags along. In the distance a trolley stands at the Thornton barrier, while in the foreground are the wires for the new Clayton barrier, which will become the 45/46 barrier when THAT moves from Tyrrel Street. Things changed almost daily from 1969 to 1971 ! Provincial House has two storeys.

A very smart 785 arrives from Clayton. Provincial House has three more storeys.

Driver training trolley 063 enters Town Hall Square. Provincial House is complete !

With Princes Way wiring incomplete, 791 from Morley Street runs across, still using the former route for the 45/46 to Town Hall Square.

Duckworth Lane Depot took over routes 45 and 46 when Thornbury ceased to have trolleys. Here 845 leaves the completed Princes Way and turns up Little Horton Lane on route 46 to Buttershaw.

PASTURE LANE 36

Route 37 City-Clayton was a slow route on account of poor road surfaces and many corners in Clayton area. The (36) City-Pasture Lane was much shorter and consequently it felt to be busier. The Pasture Lane terminus seemed accident-prone.

Pasture Lane on a good day! 833 approaches the circle from City.

The conductor pulls the frog for 727 to turn. The turning circle actually partly occupied the road junction at the end of Pasture Lane (off to the left).

Pasture Lane on a bad day. 717 has failed. With booms down she is cautiously reversed clear for 791 to pass. 753 waits behind. 727 used the circle just in time. Now the junction is blocked..

717 is hitched up to a BCT tow wagon, for a visit to Thornbury Works. It's to be hoped they take the booms down again !

Another problem at Pasture Lane was for trolleys from Clayton trying to reach the barrier. Here 838 does a full stretch.

785 runs across Pasture Lane circle from Clayton.

<u>Left</u>
The conductor pulls the frog for 793 to enter her 'new' Clayton barrier on the Town Hall Square roundabout.

<u>Below</u>
703 for Thornton passes 716 at the Clayton barrier. Since (36/37) route was soon to be converted, (45/46) had taken over the Clayton stand when Tyrrel Street and the former (45/46) barriers disappeared [see page 15].

THORNTON – THORNBURY 7

Thornton-Thornbury kept going right to the end, despite continual reorganisation of the route across the city centre. 739 turns from Hall Ings towards Town Hall Square.

At the bottom of Thornton Road, the only wires remaining are for route 7. In late winter sun in early 1972, 712 on the left heads for Thornbury, as 843 runs to Thornton.

Thornton was, for me, one of the pleasantest routes to work, though when it became cross-city it lost much of its appeal – Leeds Road and Thornbury lack the rural quality of Thornton! Looking towards Thornton, 712 turns in to the terminus. Looking the other way towards Keelham, 844 does her turn.

844 stands silently at Thornton terminus.

After due contemplation she coasts down to Spring Head Road.

Trolleybus 845 glides through Spring Head Road circle in the morning mist.

An anonymous trolley crosses the spacious route 6 turning loop.
Thornton church dominates the background.

The junction of Thornton Road and City Road, with 843 on (7) Thornton passing City Road railway goods depot on the left.

Bell Dean Road was formerly terminus for route 5. This photo shows a trolley at the site of that terminus which was obliterated when the road became dual carriageway. However it was some time later before the tramlines (which had previously been on a reserved strip) were finally covered over.

731 coasts across Four Lane Ends cross roads, from Thornton. Previously, a full circle with access from Allerton Road had existed here until inbound route 16 trolleys were diverted down West Park Road.

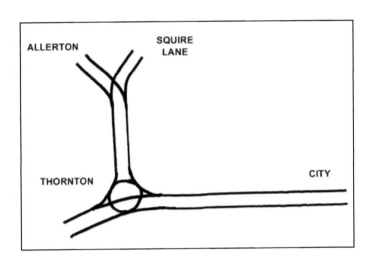

Pre-1958

With the later layout, trolleys on the '4 Four Lane Ends' short working turned via West Park Road, as seen here, and this was a popular move for enthusiasts tours.

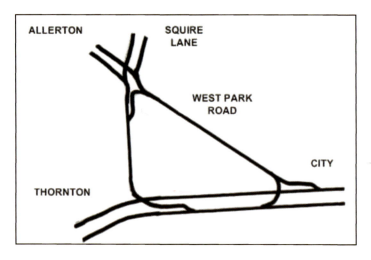

Post 1958

703 stands at Thornbury terminus. The traction poles of the outbound wires are on the right.

Completing the terminal loop via Hawthorn Street is 712. The English Electric factory forms the backdrop.

844 – MOVIE STAR !

Towards the end of trolleybus operation, a film crew turned up and used 844 as their star performer. Filming began with the shedman reversing 844 out of Duckworth Lane Depot.

Doesn't it take a lot of people to shoot a simple film?

A few clips of 844 were shot down Squire Lane.

Then to West Park Road en route to Thornton Road. Where did all the traffic come from?

Between Spring Head Road and Bell Dean Road was a favourite location to film 844, and a couple of run-pasts were made. The film crew seemed oblivious to other traffic!

842 heading for Thornton. She was totally ignored despite being almost identical to 844.

DUCKWORTH LANE

Duckworth Lane terminus was opposite the Bradford Royal Infirmary (BRI). It was normal to see at least two trolleys here, though standing time was often only a couple of minutes.

Heading for depot, a trolleybus emerges from Squire Lane to join the route 8 wires. Although not a route as such, passengers could be carried up or down Squire Lane, with BRI to Four Lane Ends being one fare stage.

Having crept out of the BRI terminus, 707 heads for City.

Making rare visits to Duckworth Lane in the last few years were rear-entrance trolleys. Here 727 nears the terminus. An AEC Regent V on service 80 appears, and the author's personal transport at that time, a Fiat Autobianchi van, waits in the foreground.

When coming from City, the access to the depot was via Toller Lane (above the roundabout) and down Little Lane. 704 passes the rear of the Old Police Station.

843 descends Little Lane, passing a bus stop for West Yorkshire services from here to Bingley. Previously this had been the stop for Hebble services to Cottingley/Bingley and to Wilsden/Hare Croft.

Although not particularly complex, the wires around Toller Lane roundabout demanded respect. The most troublesome part was the electro-frog, when City-bound. It is seen here on the left of the photo. 844 has come from depot and now heads for BRI. The other common place for dewirements was just in front of her, where the wires turned slightly left on to Duckworth Lane.

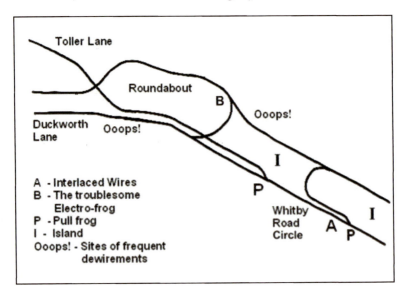

The Duckworth Lane roundabout area

A long shot along Duckworth Lane. A trolley on '8 City' swings very wide around trolleys waiting on the depot siding.

706 leads 844 on to the roundabout. 844 stops for her conductor to pull the frog to go on the long loop to depot.

735, with power off, cautiously negotiates the Troublesome Frog on the roundabout. A motorbus heading for Haworth Road emerges from Lilycroft Road.

Bathed in early summer sunshine, 730 passes 835, in dark blue, on the depot shunt loop.

707 leaves the roundabout, towards City. She is just approaching the wires of the Whitby Road circle.

A little further down 737 pauses at the Fairbank Road stop. The Whitby Road circle wires can be seen beyond the trees.

Like a drive through the woods ! On Toller Lane dual carriageway, 841 heads for Duckworth Lane.

844 passes the Old Police Station. Behind her is the depot. The wires curving right lead to Little Lane.

703 begins her descent of the 1 in 9 Whetley Hill.

Having negotiated the bend at the top of Whetley Hill, 732 inbound speeds past the end of Lincoln Road.

735 speeds down Whetley Hill. On the right, beyond the Murco sign, is the Lower Globe pub. On the left was the mouth-watering J R Smith's pork pie bakery, alas demolished.

703 arrives in White Abbey Road, and slows for the slight but tricky bend on to the dual carriageway. Whetley Hill is behind her.
Allens sarsaparilla shop is by the van on the left.

727 nears the top of Whetley Hill, heading for fresher air.

Three trolleys lurch along White Abbey Road which has always had a badly undulating road surface. White Abbey flats are on the left.

712 passes The Melborn pub at the bottom of Wood Street. Trams used to run in the centre of the road, just to either side of the islands.

735 arrives at Morrison's in Westgate. As usual a car driver thinks the bus bay is for him as well.

735 heads for BRI, passing the flattened site that will soon become the concrete monstrosity of the Yorkshire Building Society offices.

841, en route from depot to Thornbury, begins the tight turn at the City terminus of routes 8 and 16.

736 waits at the route 8 barrier in Sunbridge Road.
Trainer trolley 062 coasts down.

714 waits at the route 8 barrier.   835, in experimental livery,
arrives to follow her.

706 passes the crossing of the Allerton wires in Sunbridge Road as 844 threads her way across town, heading for Duckworth Lane depot.

At the stop above Whetley Lane crossroads, 713 outbound disgorges passengers at a site of yet more demolition.

During the late 1960s there was a shortage of trolleybus drivers. Three identical trolleys which had been in store at Thornbury for several years were 'converted' for training purposes. They were re-numbered 060, 062, 063. Here 063 circumnavigates Town Hall Square roundabout.

With ongoing overhead repairs (a broken spacer bar) a linesman encourages 731 as she free-wheels past with trolleys down.

During the final trolleybus driving test in Britain, the overhead repairs created an unexpected problem for the driver who had to perform the free-wheeling procedure. Is the linesman saying: "Sorry about this, mate. Best of luck!"

The examiner, Inspector Gobi, watches for traffic as driving instructor Arthur raises the booms. All quite legitimate – re-poling is the conductor's job, not the driver's ! This last learner-driver passed his test.

THE FINAL WEEKEND

On Friday 24 March 1972, trolleybus services in Bradford (and, indeed, in Britain) ended as trolleys from routes 7 and 8 returned to Duckworth Lane Depot. There was a large crowd waiting to see them in, standing respectfully at the sides of the yard – and blocking the main road !

The trolleys, having been cleaned and spruced up one last time by depot staff, were taken to Thornton Rd the following morning to provide special tours.

On Saturday 25 March, trolleybuses lined up on Thornton Road, from Quebec Street almost to Listerhills Road.

Nine trolleybuses were used for the tours. 842 leads.

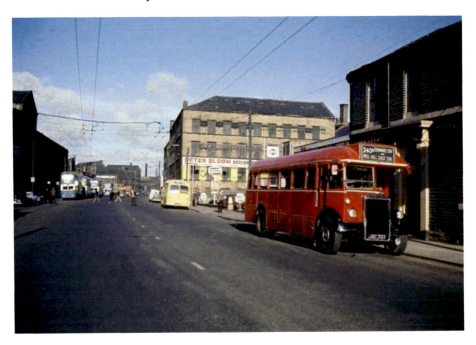

Some groups of enthusiasts came in their own preserved buses.

On tour, both 711 and 703 took a turn round the Four Lane Ends loop.

On Sunday 26 March, the convoy of trolleys left Thornbury, with 844 suitably decorated as Bradford's (on one side), Britain's (on the other side) Last Trolleybus. Here 713 follows 706 from the Works Yard, to pass the front of the depot.

With all the depot frogs removed, the through wire is now an accumulation of replacement bits. Pull-frog wires hang loose.

Preserved 758 was on display on the depot forecourt.

737, also for preservation, stayed in the yard as 844 set out on her last tour.

844 heads up the yard, her tower wagon escort stands waiting.

844 called at City Hall to collect the Mayoral party. The bells played 'Auld Lang Sein'. Several people were in tears.

844 proceeded slowly to Thornton Road, some of the crowd running ahead. The tower wagon followed close behind 'just in case'.

Another pause at the side of the Gaumont/Odeon and 844 was besieged again.

758 watches 735's return to Thornbury after her final tour.

After a trip up Thornton Road, 844 returned to Four Lane Ends, then to Duckworth Lane via Squire Lane. At the bottom of Squire Lane the Allerton wires had already been removed.

735 waits to be let in to the works. The trolleys were admitted one by one and displayed around the traverser. New AEC Swift dual-entrance buses, in three different liveries, flank the doors.

737 remains like a sentry, guarding the top of the yard.

The mayor's car and accompanying motorbuses wait for the end of the ceremony.

The closing ceremony took place in the works, with the last tour trolleys parked all around.

THE FINAL ACT

With what seemed (to enthusiasts) to be indecent haste, the remaining overhead was dismantled, ensuring that trolleybuses could never arise from their final depot. The same dedicated linesmen who had maintained the overhead, in weather fair and foul, were now required to destroy their works.

Crews worked quickly along Duckworth Lane, using all three tower wagons.

The overhead at the lower side of Toller Lane roundabout is encouraged to fall tidily. A final snip of a span completes the job.

The crews, using all three tower wagons, proceed past Duckworth depot. All the yard and internal overhead had been removed during the week. This being a Sunday morning, the yard is cluttered with the dual-entrance buses which replaced the trolleybuses.

At Duckworth Lane terminus, this lady sat patiently waiting for a number 80, while wire and fittings fell all around her!

Once on the ground, the overhead had to be cut into manageable chunks to be taken for scrap.

All the trolleybuses which were re-bodied for Bradford carried the chrome strips and the coat of arms on the lower front panel.

Several Bradford trolleybuses found sanctuary in museums. The Trolleybus Museum at Sandtoft gained a whole fleet! 834 and 845 are seen on the circuit at Sandtoft.